The World's Fastest Motorcycles

John Martin

Capstone Press

MINNEAPOLIS

Printed in the United States of America.

Capstone Press • 2440 Fernbrook Lane • Minneapolis, MN 55447

Editorial Director John Coughlan
Managing Editor John Martin
Copy Editor Theresa Early
Editorial Assistant Michelle Wood

Library of Congress Cataloging-in-Publication Data

Martin, John, 1968-
The world's fastest motorcycles / John Martin.
p. cm.-- (Wheels)
Includes bibliographical references and index.
ISBN 1-56065-208-X (lib. bdg.)
1. Motorcycles, Racing--Juvenile literature.
[1. Motorcycles.] I. Title. II. Series: Wheels (Minneapolis, Minn.)
TL442.M37 1995
629.227' 5--dc20 93-7085
CIP
AC

ISBN: 1-56065-208-X

99 98 97 96 95 94 8 7 6 5 4 3 2 1

Chapter 1

Introducing Superbikes

The motorcycles in this book are the fastest, most powerful two-wheelers around. They are the latest examples of modern motorcycle technology. Some can reach speeds of more than 230 miles (370 kilometers) per hour.

Turbochargers and **nitrous oxide boost bottles**, which allow engines to get more fuel, are what makes these bikes so fast. These devices combined with special engine tuning give the bikes amazing power. These superbikes are much faster than motorcycles you can buy from a dealer.

What Are Superbikes?

Superbikes, also called *sport bikes,* are modeled after road-racing motorcycles. In fact, some riders race their superbikes on racetracks against other superbike owners.

But superbikes are built to be driven on the road. Most superbike owners ride mainly on public streets.

Why So Fast?

You might ask, "Why would anyone want such a bike for the road? The speed limit is 65 miles (104.6 kilometers) per hour or less."

People own superbikes for the same reasons that others own sports cars. They admire the power and beauty of these high-performance machines. They do not need to race around town at top speed.

Every responsible rider knows that driving a motorcycle can be dangerous. Superbike

Mechanics tune superbikes to get them into top running condition.

owners take precautions to keep their sport as safe as possible.

Even though the superbike owner may never use the superbike's full power, everyday driving is still lots of fun.

Indian made some of the earliest superbikes.

Chapter 2

The History of Superbikes

In the 1960s people started calling fast motorcycles *superbikes*. But this type of motorcycle existed earlier.

During the 1950s companies such as Harley-Davidson, Indian, Triumph, and Norton were making some of the fastest motorcycles around.

The Norton International

The great superbike of the early 1950s was the Norton International. At first the British-made

Norton was used only for racing. Soon people wanted to own a bike just like the racers. The Norton Company added a headlight and mirrors to their bike so that it was legal for street use. Although the engine was changed to make it slower, the Norton could still reach speeds over 100 miles (160.9 kilometers) per hour.

The Japanese Superbikes

In the mid-1960s, Japanese motorcycle makers began building bikes to compete with the Americans and the British. Companies such as Honda, Suzuki, Kawasaki, and Yamaha made motorcycles that moved as fast as the Nortons and Triumphs. But the Japanese bikes had smaller, lighter engines, and were much cheaper. People who could not afford the earlier bikes now found themselves owning the new Japanese motorcycles.

The Black Bomber

One Japanese bike was Honda's CB450, nicknamed the "Black Bomber." The Black Bomber was fast. It could even beat motorcycles with larger engines. Today, motorcycle fans call the Honda CB450 the first real superbike.

During the 1970s and 1980s the Japanese made the fastest motorcycles at affordable prices. Bikes such as Suzuki's GSX1100, Honda's CB1100R and Kawasaki's GPZ1100 became common on highways around the world.

In the 1990s these motorcycles have been improved. They are still the world's fastest motorcycles.

Japanese motorcycle companies, such as Yamaha, still make the world's fastest bikes.

SHOEI
900RR
Two Brothers Racing
HONDA
H 900 RR
CBR

Chapter 3

What Makes Up a Superbike?

Superbikes have many parts in common with other motorcycles. But parts for superbikes must be lighter and stronger.

The main parts of a superbike are the **chassis**, the **fairing**, the engine, and the wheels.

The Chassis

The chassis is like a skeleton. It supports and connects the parts of the motorcycle. The handlebars and **fork legs** are linked to the

All parts on superbikes are designed for top performance.

front of the chassis. They let the rider steer the motorcycle.

On superbikes, a metal arm made of lightweight aluminum connects the rear wheel to the chassis. This metal arm and its shock absorber make up the rear suspension.

Atop the chassis sit the gasoline tank and the seat. The tank on a superbike holds about five gallons of gasoline. Seats on superbikes are made of vinyl and built for one or two riders.

The Fairing

Attached to the front and sides of the chassis is the fairing. A fairing is made of plastic, fiberglass, or carbon fiber. Its streamlined shape allows the bike to slip faster through the wind. A motorcycle with a fairing

With the added boost of nitrous oxide gas, the Team Mr. Honda/Yamaha FJ1380 can reach a top speed of 215 miles (346 kilometers) per hour.

A superbike engine viewed from above

travels up to 25 miles (40 kilometers) per hour faster than one without.

A small windshield for the rider is perched atop the fairing, and one or two headlights poke through the fairing beneath the windshield.

The Engine

Nestled inside the chassis is the engine.

Engines for superbikes are measured by their **displacement.** The displacement for most superbikes ranges from 250 to 1100 cubic centimeters (cc). The fastest bikes in this book have engines from 900cc to 1500cc. Motorcycles with larger engines usually go faster than motorcycles with smaller engines.

Superbike engines are made to produce as much horsepower as possible. To help the bike move faster, the engines are often made of lightweight metals.

At the front of the engine are the exhaust pipes. They route the hot air and smoke from the engine towards the back, away from the rider. Exhaust pipes also make the bike quieter. Sometimes they are called "mufflers" because they muffle the engine noise.

The Wheels

Attached to the metal arm of the rear suspension and to the fork legs in front are the wheels. The wheels incude tires and brakes.

A rider does a "burnout" by holding the front brake while turning the throttle.

Superbike wheels are made of lightweight metals and are smaller than other motorcycle wheels. It is easier to make sharp turns with smaller wheels.

The tires are also wider than other

motorcycle tires. This helps them grip the road better during sharp turns and quick **acceleration**.

Metal plates called **disc brakes** sit in the center of the wheel. When the rider squeezes the left hand lever or the right foot brake, pads squeeze the plates, slowing down the wheel. Friction can make the disc very hot. Some disc brakes have holes drilled in them to keep them cool.

agv
MOTUL

Chapter 4

Superbike Safety

Modern superbikes can reach dangerous speeds. But they are also safer and easier to ride than the motorcycles of the past.

Wider tires grip the road better, and new brake systems can stop the bikes in record time. The lighter weight of the new bikes also makes them easier to handle and steer.

Even with all these changes to make them safer, motorcycles can still be very dangerous. Riders who drive recklessly and without proper safety equipment are asking for injury, or even death.

SHOEI
YAMA
ZXR

The Gear

Serious superbike riders always wear full riding gear. This includes leather riding pants and jacket, gloves, boots, and a full-face helmet.

Superbike riders know the risk involved in motorcycle riding. Smart riders follow all traffic regulations and never ride without their gear.

SHOEI
MR

Chapter 5

Mr. Turbo Kawasaki ZX-11

This rocket looks like it took off at lightning speed before the paint dried. Bright red flames seem to drip from the front of the fairing toward the back of the bike.

The Mr. Turbo Kawasaki is the fastest of the fast. No motorcycle can match its speed down a **straightaway**.

To reach its top speed, the Mr. Turbo Kawasaki ZX-11 uses a turbocharger. A turbocharger compresses air and forces it into the engine. The more air an engine can get, the faster it can go.

And it really goes! The Mr. Turbo machine can reach 161 miles (259 kilometers) per hour in a quarter-mile and take only 9.27 seconds to do it.

After about a mile (1.6 kilometers), the Mr. Turbo reaches its top speed–230 miles (370.1 kilometers) per hour. This is 10 miles

The turbocharged Kawasaki ZX-11

Burnouts warm up the rear tire, and clean it, so that it grips the road better while racing.

(16 kilometers) per hour faster than the next fastest superbike. The Mr. Turbo Kawasaki really deserves to be called "the world's fastest motorcycle."

SHOEI
SPORT RIDER
MOTUL
MOTUL
MOTUL
Del Amo
GSX R
DEL AMO
plexsport

Chapter 6

RB Racing Suzuki GSXR1100 Turbo

This blue-and-white bike from RB Racing is not only one of the world's fastest motorcycles. Many riders think it is the most reliable of the superbikes as well.

The inside of the engine is completely **stock**. That means that all its parts come straight from the Suzuki factory. No special parts were added to improve its performance.

The addition of a turbocharger makes the difference. It pushes the bike to lightning-fast speed. The RB Racing Suzuki finishes the quarter-mile at 146 miles (234.95 kilometers) per hour, in just 9.87 seconds.

Its top speed is nothing to laugh at either. This turbocharged missile will accelerate up to 215 miles (345.99 kilometers) per hour.

You might think that a bike that delivers such high performance would need to be fixed all the time.

With stock parts that rarely break down, the RB Racing Suzuki GSXR1100 is probably the most reliable superbike.

The RB Racing Suzuki leans hard into a turn.

Not so! The RB Racing Suzuki rarely breaks down; when it does, spare parts are easy to find because they're Suzuki stock. It's a motorcycle fan's dream.

SHOEI
SPORT RIDER
SUZUKI
HyPerTek
DOMINATORS
DENNIS PRICE
DOMINATOR
CUSTOM PAINT
TORCO
RACING OILS
AirTech
SORCE
DUNLOP

Chapter 7

Sims & Rohm Suzuki GSXR1452

If there ever was a beauty pageant for superbikes, the Sims & Rohm Suzuki GSXR 1452 would take first place. Beautifully painted in bright pink, blue, and purple, this bike is sure to get everyone's attention. It looks like no other bike in the world.

The Sims & Rohm Suzuki uses more expensive parts than any other bike. Magnesium and titanium bolts replace the cheaper steel bolts and make the bike lighter.

Carbon fiber is used to make the gasoline tank, the fenders, and the fairing.

In the quarter-mile, the Sims & Rohm catapults its rider up to 155 miles (249.44 kilometers) per hour in the space of just 9.35 seconds.

Although it has not been officially tested, riders estimate the top speed of a Sims & Rohm to be around 220 miles (354.04 kilometers)

Superbike riders love to make their wheels scream and smoke.

The beautiful Sims & Rohm Suzuki GSXR1452

per hour. This makes it the second-fastest motorcycle in the world.

The Sims & Rohm Suzuki is more than just another pretty motorcycle.

Arai
TEAM MR.
TEAM MR.

Chapter 8

Team Mr. Honda Yamaha FJ1380

Except for the chrome mufflers that poke through behind the rider's legs, this bike looks like an everyday motorcycle.

When you look closer, you find it is not your ordinary street bike. Tucked underneath the rear **swing arm** is a small bottle that contains nitrous oxide.

Nitrous oxide is a type of gas that is fed into the engine as fuel. It gives the motorcycle an added boost of speed in fourth and fifth gear. When the nitrous hits, riders must grip the

A rider warms the back tire before blasting into a quarter-mile sprint.

handlebars firmly and brace themselves for a blast of speed.

The nitrous oxide boost bottle gives the Team Mr. Honda/Yamaha a real advantage, allowing the bike to accelerate like no other. The fastest bike over the quarter-mile, it reaches 154 miles (247.83 kilometers) per hour at that distance after only 9.25 seconds have gone by.

But the power boost does not stop at the quarter-mile. Top speed for the nitrous oxide machine is just over 214 miles (344.39 kilometers) per hour.

Reaching 154 miles per hour in 9.25 seconds, the Honda/Yamaha FJ1380 can beat any other bike in the quarter-mile.

Arai
CBR
elf
ÖHLINS
BRIDGESTONE
HONDA

Chapter 9

Two Brothers Honda CBR900RR

The Two Brothers Honda looks like a stock bike. If you put the Two Brothers Honda beside a Honda CBR900RR straight from the factory, it would be hard to tell them apart. After riding them, however, you would know the difference. This bike performs like a real racer.

The Two Brothers Honda CBR900RR has no nitrous oxide boost bottle or turbocharger. And it won't even come close to the top speeds of other bikes.

On the racetrack it is a different story. The Two Brothers Honda can make all the twists and turns of a race track seem as if they weren't even there. No other bike can keep up.

In the quarter-mile the Two Brothers Honda is almost a second slower than the other bikes. It finishes in 10.19 seconds, at 140 miles (225.30 kilometers) per hour. Top speed is only 187 miles (300.93 kilometers) per hour.

On the racetrack, the Two Brothers Honda CBR900RR turns on a dime and leaves other bikes in the dust.

The CBR900RR prepares to race.

But top speeds are not important on the race track. Racers need bikes with razor-sharp turning and quick, smooth acceleration.

What the CBR900RR does best is race. On the track no other bike can beat it.

Glossary

acceleration–increase in speed

chassis–the frame that supports the parts of a motorcycle

disc brake–a disc attached to the wheel that can be gripped to slow the wheel's spin

displacement–a measure of the size of an engine

fairing–the smooth, hard cover on the motorcycle that helps it slide through the air

fork legs–legs, split to fit over the wheel, that connect it to the chassis

nitrous oxide boost bottle–a bottle of nitrous oxide gas, used as a fuel to boost engine power

shock absorber–a device to absorb the bouncing caused by bumps and holes in the road

suspension–the system that cushions the bike as it moves over the road

stock–a part or bike that comes straight from the factory with no changes

straightaway–the straight stretch of a racetrack

swing arm–a part on the rear of a motorcycle that holds the rear wheel in place

turbocharger–a device that forces extra air into the engine and increases power

To Learn More

Friedman, Art. "Superpower Summit." *Motorcyclist*, September, 1993, 24-38.

Griffin, John Q. *Motorcycles On the Move: A Brief History.* Minneapolis, MN: Lerner Publications Company, 1976.

Ienatsch, Nick. "Unlimited Flying Ojects." *Sport Rider*, October, 1993, 16-23.

Kahaner, Ellen. *Motorcyles.* Mankato, MN: Capstone Press, 1991.

Schiller, Colin. *Fast Bikes: The New Generation.* London: Osprey Publishing Limited, 1987.

Index

Photo Credits:

Yamaha Motor Corporation: cover, p. 11; Kevin Wing: pp. 4, 7, 12, 14, 15, 16, 18, 21, 24, 26, 27, 28, 30, 31, 32, 34, 35, 36, 38, 39, 40, 42, 43; American Motorcyclist Association: p. 8; Allsport USA: p. 22.